THE

CHRISTIAN IDEA

OF

CIVIL GOVERNMENT.

NESBITT & CO., PRINTERS.

THE

CHRISTIAN IDEA

OF

CIVIL GOVERNMENT

BY

FRANCIS VINTON, D. D.

A SERMON

Preached in TRINITY CHURCH, New-York, on the occasion of the Prov. Bishop's Pastoral Letter. Repeated, by request, in GRACE CHURCH, Brooklyn Heights, and in TRINITY CHAPEL, New-York.

PUBLISHED BY PERMISSION.

NEW-YORK:
GEORGE F. NESBITT & CO., PRINTERS,
CORNER OF PEARL AND PINE STS.

1861.

SERMON.

"Put them in mind to be subject to principalities and powers; to obey magistrates." —TITUS iii, 1.

"Wherefore ye must needs be subject, not only for wrath, but for conscience sake." —ROMANS xiii, 5.

The Christian Religion prescribes the duties of men in all the relations of human life. When St. Paul instituted Titus as bishop of the Church in the island of Crete, the inspired apostle incorporated the instructions of the Holy Ghost in the Epistle to Titus, wherein political duties are enjoined among the rest: "Put them in mind to be subject to principalities and powers; to obey magistrates." So likewise, in the Epistle to the Romans, wherein God's will reveals itself in the mighty sweep of his eternal purpose towards mankind, our subjection to civil government is duly enjoined: "Let every soul be subject under the higher powers. For there is no power but of God; the powers that be are ordained of God. Whosoever therefore resisteth the power, resisteth the ordinance of God: and they that resist shall receive to themselves damnation. For rulers are not a terror to good works, but to the evil. Wilt thou then not be afraid of the power? Do that which is good and thou shalt have praise of the same: for he is the minister of God to thee for good. But if thou do that which is evil, be afraid: for he beareth not the sword in vain: for he is the minister of God, a revenger to execute wrath upon him that doeth evil. Wherefore ye must needs be subject, not only for wrath, but for conscience sake. For, for this cause pay ye tribute also; for they are God's ministers attending continually upon this very thing. Render therefore to all their dues: tribute to whom tribute is due: custom to whom custom: honor to whom honor." —(Rom. xiii, 1–8.)

It is evident from this Holy Scripture, without need of argument, that Civil Government is a Divine institution over mankind; that the magistrate is a minister of God; and that submission to established governments, and obedience to magistrates, is a religious obligation. The duty of civil obedience is made to rest on conscience, because God personally rules over the nation, in the "powers and principalities;" that is, in those abstract and fundamental principles which we call a Constitution, and in the Laws of the nation; and, by His ministers, the Magistrates of the nation. The word "ordained" expresses a definite, specific appointment—something deliberately planned and specially instituted Commentators do not differ in assigning this meaning to the term. "The powers that be are ordained of God," signifies that God governs the nation, *in* its Constitution and laws, and *by* its officers—not by his permissive will, by way of mere toleration, as He permits evil in the world; nor in virtue of the will of the people; nor by withholding His intervention: but by His positive ordinance, by His constant presence, and by His perpetual decree. Hence, the Apostle, in the text, commands a bishop in the church "to put men in mind to be subject to civil government;" because men are prone to forget their civil obligations; and because self-will, or some transient grievance, or fancied hardship, prompts to sedition and rebellion. He distinguishes "powers and principalities" from "magistrates," because those are the abstract principles embodied in the Constitution and Laws, and these are executors of the law. Hence to the Constitution and Laws of the State we must be "subject;" to the Magistrates we must be "obedient." "Put them in mind to be subject to principalities and powers, and to obey magistrates." In short, he inculcates allegiance and compliance. And he further bases these duties of loyalty on the ground of piety. "He is the minister of God to thee"—not of thee, nor from thee, but "to thee, for good." God gives authority to the civil magistrate, not man. He is "God's minister," not "the servant of the people." "And, therefore, ye must needs be subject"—necessity is laid upon you—"not only for wrath"—from fear of punishment from the sword of the magistrate—"but for conscience sake,"—as a religious duty, as an obligation of piety.

Such are the politics of St. Paul. Civil Government is a Divine institution, and is administered by Divine authority. The *mode of appointment* is indifferent. It may be by election; it may be by descent; it may be by the sword. At the time when the New Testament was written, every sort of municipal government prevailed within the circuit of the despotic rule of the Roman Empire. Yet "the powers that be are ordained of God," was a truth alike of all, exacting the same loyalty for "conscience sake." *The mode of appointment* is indifferent; but the *administration* of the government is "of God." St. Paul does not say the persons that be, but the "powers that be are ordained of God." St. Chrysostom marks this distinction in his homily on the Epistle to the Romans. "The apostle refers," says he, "not to persons, but powers." "He does not say, for there is no *ruler* but of God; but it is the thing he speaks of, and says there is no *power* but of God. And the powers that be are ordained of God." (Homily xxiii.) And this distinction is important as evincing the fallacy in that theory of Civil Government which is known as "the Divine right of Kings," and that opponent theory denominated "the Sovereignty of the People." It is a real distinction, of which the Bible gives us the illustration, in the most august transaction on record, viz.: the establishment of the Theocracy. When Jehovah took upon himself the immediate political administration of the Jewish nation, the people were summoned, and actually gave their consent. "And Moses went up to God; and the Lord called unto him out of the mountain, saying, Thus shalt thou say to the house of Jacob, and tell the children of Israel: Ye have seen what I did unto the Egyptians, and how I bore you on eagle's wings, and brought you unto myself. Now, therefore, if ye will obey my voice, indeed, and keep my covenant, then ye shall be a peculiar treasure unto me, above all people; for all the earth is mine, and ye shall be a kingdom of priests, and an holy nation. These are the words which thou shalt speak unto the children of Israel. And Moses came and called for the elders of the people, and laid before their faces all these words which the Lord commanded him. And all the people answered together, and said, All that the Lord hath spoken we will do. And Moses returned the words of the people unto the Lord." So that the Theocracy was elective; yet it was never alleged that the election gave the Theocracy its Divine authority. (See Exodus xix., 3–9.) And on the other hand, when the Jewish nation, in the time of Samuel, revolted against the political government of Jehovah—demanding "a king to judge us like all the (heathen) nations"—God did not renounce His authority, nor withhold His presence; but vindicated His unseen, but real, Sovereignty, in every subsequent vicissitude of their political fortune. (See Kings and Chronicles.) Wherefore, inasmuch as Jehovah himself abdicated the visible throne at the voice of the people, no human Potentate may claim the crown in defiance of the popular consent, by Divine right; while, on the other hand, since Jehovah demanded the assent of the nation before He visibly assumed the throne of Theocracy, it follows, that the people's Sovereignty (so-called) is all exhausted in the simple exercise of electing its rulers. The Government becomes, in either case, the Government of God; and the people are at once made "subject" under the "powers and principalities," established and instituted as Divine ordinances, in fundamental principles and laws; and are, thenceforth, bound by religious obligations, to "obey the magistrates," as "the ministers of God to them, for good."

This view of the character and authority of Civil Government represents the conscience, as the soul's eye, looking heavenward and seeing the sanction of eternal judgment vindicating the duty of political loyalty. It appeals to the conscience, as the judicial faculty of the soul, to determine the moral obligation of submission and of obedience to the constituted authorities of the State. It elevates politics among the interests of man, along with ethics, and flings around the Civil Government of a nation the sacredness of the Divine Presence, and the authority of Almighty God. This is the religious aspect of Civil Government.

But there is, furthermore, the Christian aspect; and this is embraced in the words of the Lord Jesus Christ, after his Resurrection: "All power is given unto Me, in Heaven and *in earth.*" (Matt. xxviii, 18.) He is the only Sovereign, "the King of Kings, and Lord of Lords." Wherefore, the authority of Civil

Government, which, in the Bible, is ascribed to God, is lodged in the Person of the Lord Jesus Christ, as the token of the higher Christian civilization to which nations should attain under the dispensation of the Gospel. As in the Religious aspect, so in the Christian aspect; national life is organic, and the Nation is an organic body. Jesus Christ is the Head, from whom the Body derives its life, its nourishment, and its growth. The Constitution of a nation makes it a unit, and organizes its members into a corporation. Man is developed therein to his fullest capacity; for it is society that developes man, and the Christian nation is the highest type of society; for as the body is one, and hath many members, and all the members of that one body, being many, are one body, so also is the Nation; and the eye cannot say unto the hand, I have no need of thee; nor the hand to the feet, I have no need of you; but God has set the members, every one of them, in the body as it has pleased Him, that there should be no schism, nor, much less, "*secession*," in the body; but that the members should have the same care, one for another, and whether one member suffer, all the members suffer with it; or one member be honored, all the members rejoice with it. (See 1 Cor., xii, 12–26.)

This is the aspect of Society in the organic relations of National being. Individualism is recognized, but in its associations. Alone, man would perish, like a limb cut off. And as the individual man is the product of society in the family, so the true and natural development of man is in society, of which the Christian nation is the Divine organism and highest exponent, for man's terrestrial life and happiness.

In opposition to this DIVINE IDEA of the Nation, is the theory of the SOCIAL COMPACT. When the rulers in the Church, and the rulers in the State, perverted the Scripture by confounding the distinction between the "powers" and the persons in the Government, the Divine right of kings, in the line of hereditary descent, became a personal prerogative of absolute power. Nations were regarded as made for kings, and not kings for the nations. It was the saturnalia of royalty, amid the groanings of the populace. But when the imprisoned soul burst its shackles, and hurled them at its oppressor in the Vatican, proclaiming freedom in religion, there sprang, also, a protestantism in politics. At length it assumed the dignity of a philosophy, under the tuition of Locke, who published the theory of "the Social Compact." According to this philosopher, Society originated in a mutual agreement among individuals: magistrates derived their powers from the gift and appointment of the people: allegiance to the government was based on interest and selfish safety: Society was but an aggregation of single persons; a conglomerate and not an organic thing: revolution was not only a right but a law: and majorities were supreme, while minorities were powerless. This theory of the Social Compact took root in France, where the pupils of Locke outran the precepts of their master, and enacted the bloody scenes of political tragedy with which the awful history of the French Revolution has made us familiar.*

The philosophy of Locke was materialism. Bald and haggard, it had no spiritual beauty. Deriving all knowledge from the outward world; denying intuitive ideas, and dignifying the senses as the only channels of truth, that miserable philosophy left no place for spiritual facts, and utterly ignored the rule and presence of God in the world. It professed respect for the second table of the law, but put the first table out of sight. It was negatively atheistic, and worked out practical atheism in society. As a corollary in civil government, it decried capital punishment; because the magistrate, being endowed with no Divine vicegerency, but merely a fellow-citizen, was invested with no authority over the life of man. And yet, with singular inconsistency, it gave

---

NOTE.—Locke was born in 1632, and died in 1704. As a proof of the *good* influence of the philosophy of Locke, historians attribute the settlement of the British Constitution, at the Revolution in 1688, largely to the principles and maxims of that philosopher. But as an instance both of the arrogancy and weakness of Locke, as a practical civilian, the fate of his political Constitution for South Carolina is significant. In 1669, the "Proprietaries" of South Carolina applied to LOCKE and SHAFTESBURY for a Constitution for the colony. It was a queer medley; providing for a "nobility" of "Palatines," "Landgraves," and "Caciques," with biennial assemblies of the Legislature. It was promulgated by its author, (Locke,) as "immortal." It was abrogated by the Proprietaries themselves, in April, 1693, after a life of less than a quarter of a century. It left the system of "biennial assemblies," with slight changes, as the only relic of that "social compact;" unless we say it bequeathed a traditional and chronic discontent with existing governments, and a disposition to make fresh experiments in constitutions. As the Huguenots "were fully enfranchised, as though they had been free-born citizens," May 1, 1691, (Statutes II., 58–60, S. C.,) it is probable that they were instrumental in overturning the "fundamental constitution," so soon as they had acquired political power. See Bancroft's History U. S., vol. III., pp. 10–16.

scope to the political passions to legalize murder for political opinions. It was seeming philanthropy, but real cruelty. It professed to inculcate the rights of man, yet admitted no Divinity, therefore, no charity, in its composition. It had no authority but the caprice of self-will, and in the motives of self-interest. Change and revolution were its rule. Subjection and obedience for conscience sake had no place in its ethics. God and conscience were obliterated.

The hoary dogma of the "divine right of kings," and the popular demand of the right of "self-government," with many inconsistencies and extravagant claims on either side, came into collision. These two opponent systems battled for years in Europe. There seemed to be no point of coalescence, until the English Revolution perfected the British Constitution, and a Constitutional monarch presided over the destinies of the British Empire. The Constitution became the principality and sovereign power—the king, the chief magistrate. Submission to the Constitution was the duty alike of king and subject; while obedience to the magistrate was the token of the loyalty of the people. The right of revolution was the *ultima ratio*—the exception, not the rule—of liberty. And this right was founded not in self-will, but in duty to the will of God, as embodied in the Constitution of the British nation.

Our Fathers acted on this principle in the American Revolution: maintaining the Constitution of the British empire, in antagonism to a faithless Ministry. The Patriots of our Revolution were the true Loyalists, not rebels. In resisting the Cabinet, they contended for the supremacy of the Constitution of the British nation. They were "subject" unto "principalities and powers" for conscience sake, while denouncing the necessity of disobeying "magistrates."

On the principle of Constitutional Liberty, our fathers established the Government of these United States. The Federal Constitution is the type and the organic instrument of national life. The magistrate under that Constitution is "the minister of God to thee," to me, to all our countrymen, "for good." The old "Confederation" was an abortive experiment of the Compact of States. It resulted in imbecility. The theory of the social compact has been tried and condemned. It has produced imbecility, anarchy and woe. Its principle of individual liberty is, however, embalmed in the fact of a free, consolidated Republic.

The theory of a promiscuous conglomeration of men, miscalled society, is false in history, faithless in its principles, weak and self-destructive in its execution, and is among the phantasies of the past hour. Where it is galvanized into ghastly imitations of life, it is too horrid in its grimaces of freedom to engage the affections of any lover of Liberty and Law. Demagogues and religionists attempt now and then the revolting experiment.

I was wrong when I said these counterfeits of liberty are past. For, since that sentence was penned, the newspapers have reported the words of a noted Abolitionist and boastful Independent—a man of acknowledged talent, of wide influence for his private virtues, and of some authority among a class of our fellow-citizens—a Representative man, therefore, or I would not think it seeming, in this house, on this occasion, to quote his words—who, as the orator at the late Puritan festival in Philadelphia, on "Forefathers' Day," so called, pronounced with applause these words: "Men need governments of restraint only as they are not developed and not free. As the individual becomes educated and strong in his whole nature, moral and intellectual, he needs no government, for God made the human soul sufficient for all its own exigencies. It is a perfect state. It is competent to entire sovereignty." *

These statements are put forth as the latest results of the cardinal doctrines of Puritan theology, and Puritan ethics, and Puritan politics. According to them, in Heaven, where man is perfect, there is *no government.* But to the Christian's faith in Holy Scripture, such sentiments are shocking for their blasphemy. To a sinful man's humility, they are offensive for their arrogance. To a patriot's loyalty, they are deserving of denunciation, as contravening all law, and as expressing the demoniac spirit of anarchy. Each man may "do that which is right in his own eyes."

It is a singular example of the coalescence of extremes in

---

*H. W. Beecher's Oration in Philadelphia, Dec. 22, 1860.

fanaticism, that these Puritan Abolition sentiments of the North, and the self-willed Secessionist doctrines of the South, are practically one thing: grounded in the same vicious philosophy, producing the same fruits of sedition and rebellion, and shaking hands in an unholy alliance of hostility against the organic Constitution of the Nation. For the law of our Union represses the vagaries of selfishness. Whether it be the individual man or the individual State, the Word of God in Holy Scripture, and the teaching of the Episcopal Church in this land, unite in enjoining loyalty on every citizen, as the pious obligation on the conscience of the Christian.

The people of these United States, under the Federal Constitution, are ONE NATION, organic, corporate, divinely established, subject to government, and bound in conscience to obedience. Disloyalty to the Constitution, is, therefore, impiety toward God. Revolution is not justifiable, except in extreme oppression. Only where "life, liberty, and the pursuit of happiness" are positively hindered, does our American Declaration of Independence justify revolution. In no other emergency is subjection to the Constitution and obedience to the magistrate superseded by any higher law of obedience to God. To destroy this Union, therefore, is to commit a sin, which God will righteously punish by evils which no prescience can foresee, and no wisdom can repair. "Lawfully to secede" is a self-contradiction, a solecism. Secession is disunion, and Disunion is Treason; for, the CONSTITUTION abides as our "principality and power" "ordained of God," securing Life, Liberty, and Happiness to the Nation.

There is, therefore, but one thing to do in the exigency of the Republic. That thing is for the magistrate "who beareth not the sword in vain" to execute the laws; and for the citizen to obey, and be subject to "the powers that be." But for the present distress there needs forbearance, with honest endeavor to redress real, or even fancied, grievances; to silence just complaints; and to reconstruct National intercourse into a more perfect harmony of confidence with patience and mutual love and prayer for one another, among the fellow-citizens of our Nation. By confessing and obeying Jesus Christ as our Sovereign, we shall be united again in heart, and be a model among the kingdoms of the world. But disloyal to Him, we shall be scattered and peeled—a dismembered body, a reproach and a hissing, and a byeword among the nations.

Thanks be to the long-suffering and blessing of our God, we have lived and prospered as fellow-citizens of the United States, under a National Constitution. But, destroy the Union, we are dead. And the ruins of the noblest Temple that political wisdom, guided and inspired by God's Word, has ever reared around the altars of Liberty and Law, for the protection and for the development of man, shall, in times to come, be visited by our degenerated posterity of pigmy children; who shall gaze upon the shattered, colossal fragments of our Constitution with stupid wonder at the greatness of their forefathers, and with muttered curses against the suicidal treason of this generation, who deprived themselves of a secure Home; who exiled their offspring to vagrancy and despair; and who blasted the blooming expectations of Humanity, just as the fruit of Constitutional Liberty was becoming set in the Tree of political life in the midst of Europe, among the civilized nations of the Earth.

www.ingramcontent.com/pod-product-compliance
Lightning Source LLC
LaVergne TN
LVHW020644110826
845149LV00004B/1349

* 9 7 8 1 4 1 8 1 8 9 4 9 5 *